This book is dedicated in loving memory of my grandmother, Linnie Keys, and grandfather, Albert Smith. Thank you both for always providing a home for me to come to. To my grandmother, Clarebelle Smith, thank you for your love and support. The lessons that you all have taught me are invaluable and I honor you all by passing on the love that you gave me.

To my parents, Cal and Linda. I love you and I am so glad that you came together to create me.

This book is also dedicated to every person who has a dream but seems to be stuck in a pattern. May God grant you the strength and courage to move forward with his wonderful and beautiful plan for your life.

Foremost to God, I love you. I thank you, for never giving up on me and always bringing me back to where I need to be. Your love is immense and I feel it every day! Thank you!

Acknowledgments

I would first like to acknowledge my loving husband, Owolabi Alaba, for never failing to be that rock that I could lean on in good and bad times. You remembered me when I forgot who I was. Thank you for your patience as I rediscovered myself and the purpose God has for me.

I would like to express my love and gratitude to my daughters. Ariel, thank you for your example of strength and discipline and for believing in me even though you didn't understand the process. Your existence has taught me to trust in God more than any person in my life. Thank you! Yemi, thank you for your love and enthusiasm in every adventure we embark on. Your kind spirit is contagious. I love you. Dayo, thank you for keeping me in the moment and helping me to remember what's important.

Special thanks to my friends. Tracey Smith, for helping me to understand myself better through our friendship. Thea Camera, for showing me that it is never too late to follow our dreams.

To Aunt Lashaune and Granny Hogan, thank you for being spiritual mothers to me. I am so blessed that God put you in my life.

To my sisters, Juanakee and Brittinay, for their courageous example in moving to a new place and making their mark on their own terms. To my sister, Qianna, I am empowered by your perseverance and determination. Your courage has emboldened me. I thank you!

To my brother, Dejuan, for showing me that it is never too late to get it right. I love you!

To my nieces and nephews, you are amazing. I think of you daily and I am blessed to be your aunt.

Special thanks also to my editor Laurel Ornitz; your deadlines and encouragement were just what I needed to complete this project.

Life is a process and we get a chance every day to renew ourselves.

Foreword

This book was born out of an uncomfortable growth period in my life. As a young person, I found my calling early in life. I was called to help people heal from the trauma of life. My calling led me to pursue a psychology degree and become a counselor. After many years of operating a successful counseling center for families and children, I had a life-changing experience that called me to question my calling and my life's purpose. I recall this day like no other in my life.

It had been snowing in Chicago, which was usual for that time of the year. My girls were out of school due to a snow day, but I decided to go to the office just to check in. As I was leaving my home, I was hit in my driver's side by a car that slid out of control. Although I immediately felt pain after being hit, I tried to shake this off and keep things moving, but over the next days and weeks, I would discover how badly that crash injured my back. I did all the things good Christians are supposed to do: I prayed and claimed my healing. But my back pain became worse as the weeks went on. Eventually, I closed my center and had to let several employees go. I was devastated to say the least. My finances were left in a state of shock and awe. To make matters worse, my recovery would cause me to have to depend on my children and husband for help to do the most mundane tasks such as grocery shopping and carrying things up and down the stairs. I missed many of the children's school events and family outings. I was 35 years old and stuck in the body of a non-mobile 90-year-old.

During this time, I was challenged to see myself in a new way. I had to learn that I was not my business. But who was I? My identity had become entangled in my company. I lost many friends during this time. I no longer could afford the fancy lunches and traveling on a whim. Also, it seems I was not so interesting to talk to anymore. Over time, I came to realize that God can heal and I began to walk daily and to claim my healing. I am thankful to say that I am healed today. God restored me. During this period of my life, I learned many things about myself. I learned that I had become rigid in what I tried or what I was open to. I also learned that my financial situation would not have been so devastating had I listened to my inner voice. You know that voice that speaks to you when you are moving too fast or making decisions out of fear. This experience has taught me to listen to the spirit within me.

By the time I was able and ready to hit the road again, the employment market was very tight. I discovered that entering the workplace was not as easy as I thought it would be. I had been an entrepreneur most of my career and found it difficult to get a full-time job, although I had excellent skills and a great work ethic. My finances were in such a mess that I felt I needed a job to meet my daily needs and self-employment did not seem like a valid option.

God has a plan for us. He knew I needed to slow down and practice what I was preaching. I needed to attend to the affairs of my own home. I needed to find balance in a life that was so unbalanced. I needed to get in touch with my creator and build an intimate relationship with him. Over the years, I had become routine in my prayers. I had stopped seeking God as a father but more of a genie in a bottle who could provide more things.

But I knew God was preparing me for something. So during this period of time I decided to open myself to life and all the goodness it had for me. I did things out of love and not fear. In this book, you will discover the very things that I did to rediscover my purpose, passion, and self-worth and to get my life back, and how you can apply these things to your own life.

Life's hardships can knock you down and make you feel that maybe you were not meant for greatness. Maybe achieving and living a life of purpose is for someone else. I challenge you to claim your victory and to take steps every day that renew and motivate you to get what God has for you. You have everything you need to be successful right now. The Lord has designed and blessed you to be a blessing. So go get what God has for you!

The one thing I learned for certain on this journey is that when we are stuck, held captive by our yesterdays, we cannot live fully in our present or plan for our future. We become focused on ourselves and miss opportunities to give to others and our communities. When we linger too long in a place of unworthiness, doubt, and what-ifs, we miss out on all of the beauty and glory that this life has in store for us. This book was designed to move you forward into a better place so that you can write a new script for your life just like I did. Use it to motivate and push you into truly living with purpose and doing what God has called you to do. Remember every day is a new beginning and chance to get it right. I love you and can't wait to hear about your journey. You can write to me at Melisa@melisaalaba.com.

MELISA ALABA

As we embark on this journey, you will discover some new things about yourself. You will begin to operate from your authentic self, that part of you that knows the truth and acts on it.

But how do you do these things when you are lost? When you have given so much of yourself to your husband, children, work, or friends that you don't even know who you are? You start by dedicating a small amount of time daily to get to know yourself. God promises to teach and counsel you in Psalm 32:8. Ask God to come in and to reveal truth to you every day as you gain wisdom and knowledge in doing the exercises in this book.

Through personal experience and working with hundreds of clients over the years, I have found that there are 11 principles that we need to understand to move forward in our lives. You will find that each "mindful idea" reflects a principle that you need to master. Each of the 52 chapters in this book is divided among the 11 principles and correlates to the 52 weeks of the year with a mindful idea for each week. You can use this book sequentially from one week to the next or choose the exercise or practice that speaks to you the most at the time.

Each week jump into one of the exercises that will allow you to learn about yourself and what God really has in store for you. The activities are simple yet powerful. You will be amazed at how God will speak to you through simple acts. It's OK if you skip a day or two, but get back in there and remember every day we have an opportunity to renew and rejuvenate ourselves. During my transition time, I realized that it did not take a lot of material things to make me happy. I would have loved to travel around the world during this time, but to be honest, I was fortunate if I could go to a matinee to see a movie. I learned to enjoy the simple joys of life and to be in the moment. Oh what a joy to be at my daughter's basketball game and to really watch each move rather than on my cell phone checking in with employees or meetings. I learned to appreciate the colors of leaves in the fall and spring. I took long walks on trails. I relaxed and became unhurried and unrushed. I took in new breath and you can too. This journey will have a big effect on how you see yourself and this life that we are leading. Give yourself permission to be brave, confident, courageous, and vibrant—yes this can be you!

These words embody the 11 keys to living a fully aware life: *abundance, acceptance, balance, commitment, connection, discovery, forgiveness, giving, gratitude, organization,* and *purpose.* Over the years, I have found that in order to live up to our fullest potential we have to embody these key concepts into our life. When we do, we become more aware of our presence on earth and how our existence has a purpose greater than we can imagine. But in order to get to this special place we have to slow down and breathe. I pray that you do just that. This book was designed for you to engage in the ideas individually, with a friend, or in a group. Have fun with it. Reflect on the questions at the end of each exercise. Keep a journal as you do each exercise from week to week. Notice your personal growth as you go on this journey.

At times we wander through daily living unaware of all the lessons that show up in the classroom of our experience. I encourage you to take time to be mindful of all the classes that living has afforded you.

"Our deepest fear is not that we are inadequate. Our deepest fear is that we are powerful beyond measure. It is our light, not our darkness, that most frightens us. We ask ourselves, who am I to be brilliant, gorgeous, talented, fabulous? Actually, who are you not to be? You are a child of God. Your playing small does not serve the world. There is nothing enlightened about shrinking so that other people won't feel insecure around you. We are all meant to shine, as children do. We were born to make manifest the glory of God that is within us. It's not just in some of us; it's in everyone. And as we let our own light shine, we unconsciously give other people permission to do the same. As we are liberated from our own fear, our presence automatically liberates others."

—MARIANNE WILLIAMSON,
A Return to Love: Reflections on the Principles of "A Course in Miracles"

Contents

1

Abundance

"Abundance is not something we acquire.
It is something we tune into."

—WAYNE DYER

WEEK 1

Create a vision board

Creating your vision board is a powerful tool in getting unstuck and clear about your purpose and dreams. Creating a vision board will assist you in making a visual vision statement for your life. The concept is that your mind will direct the things that you placed on your board to come your way. Many people first heard of vision boards when the book *The Secret* by Rhonda Byrne came out years ago. However, the idea of creating a vision board is not new. The biblical scripture, Habbakuk 2:2 states: write the vision and make it clear. God wants us to have a vision for our lives. Clearly God wants us to have a vision for our life.

I have been using some form of a vision board since 2001 with great success. The vision board that I created in 2009 is the most memorable because it served as a catalyst of restoring my dreams and hopes. The vision board I created that summer helped me to see that I really did have a future and that it was purposeful and bright. Every dream that I had locked away I pulled it out and placed it on that board. To my amazement several years later I have accomplished many of things revealed during my darkest hour. Vision Boards are fantastic when used correctly in helping you expand your vision and open up to the abundant possibilities that life has to offer. Over the years, I have also heard people complain that they have never received what they hoped for. Here are a few strategies to seeing your dreams fulfilled.

Before creating your board, allow yourself plenty of time and space to focus on your dreams and goals. As the designer, you become creative as you cut out pictures of what you want to see in your life and glue or tape them to a poster board. Really think about what you want to see in your life. Ask yourself questions such as: How will accomplishing this change my life? What does my spirit long for but I fear doing or having? What is the purpose that God has for me?

Become clear about who you are and what you want. Be authentic in what you want to see happen. Choose pictures that reflect your true self. If you choose cars and homes that you really do not desire, then you will not manifest it. This is a common mistake that many people make when creating a vision board. They choose pictures that are not in alignment with their spirit. Choose pictures that you are drawn to. They may be abstract, colorful, or symbolic. Ask yourself: What do I really want? Free yourself up to fantasize about living a no-limit life. What is calling me? Oftentimes, our spirit will direct us to something we would not have chosen ourselves but we know deep down it has significance.

Create your board based on your values in every area of your life. Think about your health, spirit, family, business, career, recreation, and your finances. There are many types of boards such as financial boards, business boards, and all-in-one boards. No matter which board you choose, always remember to use your values as starting points in the creation process. What would success look like to you? Would it include time for your family and friends? What are my values? How will I reflect that in my future?

Use meditation, prayer, and affirmations to move your spirit in direct alignment with what you want to manifest. Are you ready to receive all that you asked for? Would you believe it if it happened? Take time to prepare for the manifestation, and truth will be revealed to you at an accelerated pace.

Lastly and probably most importantly, take action. When opportunities in the form of people or situations come your way, go for it. You can only achieve your goals and dreams if you put in the time and work. Your spiritual self wants to move and is aching for something to achieve. You have to be the catalyst to get the ball in action. Every time you reach higher, God will expand that reach. Make this the year that you give him something to work with!

What hidden dreams did you discover from creating your vision board? What shifts in your perspective are you aware of now?

Journal Notes

WEEK 2

Give from a place of abundance

I have often heard people say, "I would do more if I had more money." Oftentimes we do not realize that we have more than enough to sustain us and to live a life of abundance. My pastor, Dr. Bill Winston, likes to tell the story of when he and his wife were managing their finances as a young couple. He recalls how his wife, Dr. Veronica Winston, would make soup to help others. Even though they were not where they wanted to be financially, they gave from their abundance. She was creative in giving to others. She gave to others because she knew in her spirit that she was rich. She was rich with God's resources, and when you are wealthy, you can never be broke. I believe many people do not give because they do not truly understand the value of the resources that they possess. Understanding that abundance is a manifestation of our thoughts and actions is an important concept. In order to be truly abundant, we must use faith and action to support our beliefs.

It is also important to give to those that you want to bless, not that you feel obligated to bless. Giving from a state of obligation or guilt will cause you to feel anger and resentment. So make sure that when you give to anyone or any cause it's rooted in love. Other times we do not give because we feel that we should be paid for all the services we render. Payment for our services or goods often reflects the value we place on our time and talent. Money is a good and necessary part of living in our society. We require money to function in this world. However, we are sowing an abundant seed into our future when we give from our own resources, which include our talents and time.

Almost weekly I choose to bless several people with life coaching actions to help them achieve their dreams and goals. I do this out of love. I also want to be a blessing to those who need someone who needs someone to talk to who may not be able to afford my services at the time but need my assistance. Because I give from a place of love and not desperation, God rewards me with abundance in my business and personal life. I always have more than enough.

This week begin to journal about your abundance. I am sure you have an overflow of treasures in your kitchen cabinet, bedroom closets, and pouring out of your garage. Living in abundance is a way of being. What can you give to someone out of the spirit of love this week? How did it feel to freely give without being asked?

Those who have an abundant mentality are easily recognized because they manifest the good in every situation. How can you demonstrate your abundance this week? What resources do you possess that will help someone else?

Journal Notes

WEEK 3

Create positive affirmations

Affirmations are designed to bring forth our innermost thoughts and feelings. Many times we say affirmations in the reverse. We might say "I am sick," "I am fat," "I am stupid," and "I am having a bad day." As surely as we say it, the indications or symptoms begin showing up in our life to prove these statements true. I am asking you to use affirmations to bring forth those things you deeply desire or attributes you require to do what you were called to do.

It is not necessary that each affirmation be present in your life right now. However, it is vital that you use words to bring forth what you believe to be true. The evidence will begin to show as you call these things out. Psalm 18:21 states that death and life are in the power of the tongue, and they that love it shall eat the fruit thereof. This simply means that we can bless or curse ourselves with our own words.

A few years ago, as a last resort, I decided to use affirmations with my middle child. I had just had a baby and had very little energy or time to sit with her while she did her homework. This was my child that always required more time and attention. She would often leave her books at school or forget assignments. So I spent a lot of time assisting her with tedious tasks before she could begin her assignments. Out of frustration, I had her repeat these statements in the morning. She would say, "I am well organized," "I am an honor roll student," "I am a good citizen." Soon she started excelling at school. It was so exciting that I almost didn't believe it. Because I had helped her for so long, I was astounded that she was now doing her own assignments and remembering to bring her books home daily. The best part is that her self-esteem rose. She now knew she could excel. What a powerful lesson for me and her. Affirmations work and are powerful tools. To bring forth blessings and abundance in any area of your life, use affirmations. They work.

Write a list of affirmations that reflect what you would like to see in your life. Here are a few to get you started:

- I attract positive people in my life.
- I stop eating when I am full.
- I prefer fruits and veggies in my diet.
- I look great.
- God has a wonderful plan for my life.
- I am wonderfully made in his image.
- I lead an active lifestyle.
- I am a resourceful person.
- I am focused.
- I complete tasks easily.

- I am organized.
- I am financially savvy.
- My bank account is multiplying.
- I have everything I need right now to lead a successful life.

Which statements will you use to affirm yourself? How will you use affirmations to affirm those around you? Have you ever affirmed the negative and seen it manifest?

Journal
Notes

WEEK 4
List your talents

Ask yourself, "How am I using my talents?" and "What resources do I need to share my talents?" If you feel that you are lacking something to complete your task, ask God to show you what you need right now. I understand firsthand how depressing it can be to feel that you lack the resources to effectively bring your gift to life. A few years ago, while seeking employment, I decided to start writing. So while sending out my resume, interviewing, and following up with potential employers, I wrote. I knew I had a message although I didn't have an audience or income to publish a book. However, I decided to trust God enough to pursue writing. I started slowly with a free blog site. Soon I began to see that I really did have something to say and it felt empowering just to write. Although unemployment was no walk in the park, I know it was a gift from God, because I was in the perfect situation to further develop my talent. According to Proverb 19:6, our gifts will bring us before great men. God has richly blessed you with an abundance of gifts and talents.

Take inventory of your resources and begin to map out how you will move on the plans the Lord has for you. What talents do you have that you can perfect right now? Take a few minutes and list your talents. Society values talents like singing, acting, and dancing, but all talents are needed in our lives. Maybe you have a special gift for taking care of young children or you may have a calling to connect with the elderly. Chances are you use your talents every day but have never taken the time to determine how you can use them to help others outside of your immediate family. As a life coach, I have encountered numerous clients who had a difficult time identifying their talents and gifts. Here are a few questions to ask yourself in determining your talents. What do other people often ask me to do? What role do you often find yourself in when in a group or organization? What activities are you drawn to in your free time? What would you do if you had more time? When you were growing up, what careers were suggested to you by your teachers?

I remember my business teacher from high school saying that I would make a great teacher one day. I had never thought of myself as a teacher, but here I am many years later a teacher. That teacher had recognized my gift because he understood the qualities that are needed to excel at teaching. He noticed the qualities of leadership, a giving nature, and the desire to see others succeed.

Many times we wait for the perfect situation, but the time is ripe now. Start pursuing your purpose and passion today. Use whatever resources you have in this present moment. As Pastor T. D. Jakes often preaches, "Work that thing," referring to our gifts and talents. Working your gift daily is the perfect setup for opportunity to show up. When the door of opportunity knocks, will you be ready? Take inventory of your resources and begin to map out how you will move on the plans that the Lord has for you.

What resources do you have right now to pursue your passion? How can you schedule your time to work on your goal? What information do you need to make your dream manifest?

Journal Notes

WEEK 5

Be a problem solver

Put complaining on hold and become a problem solver. It is difficult and nearly impossible to create or accept abundance in your life if you are always complaining. In life there will be problems and I guarantee when you step out on faith to do something new you will face challenges. It is very easy to complain when things get tough or you feel as if you are having some bad breaks. Each day this week work to focus on solutions. Accept that the problem is real. Visualize it. Then begin to brainstorm five different ways to handle it. Soon you will realize that some problems offer great opportunities in life.

When I reflect back on the car accident that I had in 2008, I am grateful for the opportunities that it offered to me. Through that very painful situation, God brought me to my greater purpose. I have had the opportunity to teach others about the power of meditation and learn about our divine ability to heal ourselves.

Have you ever noticed that no matter where you go you may find people who complain endlessly about everything? Most times they are simple things, but complaints magnify the significance of the problem. This week commit to being a problem solver. Each time a problem appears, big or small, think of ways to solve it. Learn to be creative in your environment. You may notice that applying this principle will change your outlook and the internal process of the way you see life.

Reflect on your past. What situations have you had that turned into learning opportunities?

What skills do you need to become a good problem solver? What challenges did you have this week? How did you deal with them?

Journal Notes

2

Acceptance

"*Acceptance is not love. You love a person because he or she has lovable traits, but you accept everybody just because they're alive and human.*"

—ALBERT ELLIS

A ffirmations:
I choose to accept myself with all my beauty and flaws. I choose to accept my neighbors with all of their beauty and flaws.

WEEK 6

Accept people for who they are

Accept people for who they are and love them in that moment. Many relationships are destroyed because of the refusal to accept one another. Sit back, breathe, and think of the good qualities that people in your life have and what they bring to the table. Then relax and enjoy them. Life is ebb and flow, it has balance, and there will be a time when it may seem that everything is unsteady and a quality that you lack will be required and will show up in your relationship. We are all on a journey and God is patient with us all, so why are we so impatient with each other? Often the very thing that annoys us about our sister, friend, or spouse is a reflection of something we see in ourselves.

The Rain Meditation is a wonderful way to begin to accept others in their present state. The acronym RAIN means the following: R (Recognize what is happening), A (Allow life to be just as it is), I (Investigate your inner experience), and N (Non-identification). Part of the Buddhist tradition, the Rain Meditation has come to represent a way for us to accept life as it presents itself in the moment.

Ask yourself: Do I want this person to change for their good or is there another motive? Am I seeking their growth to serve me and my needs? If it is truly for that person, then encourage them—then love them just as they are.

Journal Notes

WEEK 7

Say your name!

S ay your name! Yes really say your name. Fill in the blanks with your name.

_____

You are so cool, cute, funny, fun, wise, smart, and I like you.

This week focus on saying your name and examining who you are. You may be called wife, mom, sister, aunt, friend, and that is all wonderful. But who do you say you are? First and foremost, you are a child of God. You are love because God loves you.

I believe we were all created with a divine purpose. Yet we are loved by God whether we choose to pursue it or not. His love for us is unconditional. You are who God has called us to be. You are more than a role or a title; you are a representative of Christ. So go ahead and say your name. When we understand that God loves us just because we exist, then we can truly be free to walk in our light. Accept yourself as a child of God.

What does unconditional love mean to you? How does love manifest itself in your life? What are some ways you can begin to show love and kindness to yourself and to others? We are all children of God.

Journal Notes

WEEK 8

Do it their way

Sometimes we need to go with the flow. Let your friends pick the restaurant. You may find you like it. I am accustomed to being the planner in my family. I usually get a little uptight when things are not organized well and then I go in to save the day. The older we become, the easier it is to become stuck in routines and rituals.

Recently, one of my sisters planned a family event. Then at the last minute she changed the plan entirely. At first I was annoyed but I decided to take my own challenge and to go with the flow. We met at a popular skating rink in Atlanta, Cascades. I showed up with a good attitude determined to have a good time and I did. In fact it was one of our best family outings ever. We skated, laughed, and talked. My mom even got on the skating floor. That was a sight to see. I am so glad we all had that experience. Letting go can not only change your perceptions but it can also enlighten and empower others around you. Because I allowed my sister to plan her event, she was able to take ownership over its success. Now I am looking forward to the next event that she plans. It's never too late to try something new.

Pick one person this week and allow them to take the lead. Be a willing participant in their event. How did it feel? Did you feel less rigid, more accepting? Did you learn something new? What feeling do you notice as you begin contemplating letting go?

3

Balance

"Life is like riding a bicycle. To keep your balance you must keep moving."

—ALBERT EINSTEIN

WEEK 9
Eat to live

In the United States we suffer from many ailments because of poor eating habits. Dr. Furham, the author of *Eating to Live,* is one of the leading medical professionals advocating the benefits of eating foods that heal.

We are often bombarded with stress-producing activity in our society. Many times this leads to eating on the go, working long hours, and spending countless time in front of the television. Science is beginning to understand the impact of fast food in our bodies. Many of our poor eating habits can be linked to illnesses that cause us to use prescription drugs. Jeff, from the Herb Shop of Vinings, contends that we often lack the essential minerals and vitamins to keep us healthy. He says that once we start to support our immune system with the necessary foods, minerals, and vitamins, we will notice a significant change in our overall well-being.

I have suffered with allergies for years. But a few years ago I began to change my diet and miraculously my allergies lessoned. I also began taking preventative measures to keep my sinuses clear. Thanks to Dr. Oz, the Neti Pot has helped me reduce the amount of sinus infections that I get. I went from having four to six sinus infections a year to less than two per year. If I had not decided to get serious about my health, I would have continued to suffer.

Many times we keep our promises to others, but we somehow fail ourselves. Your health and well-being is worth fighting for. I encourage you to put yourself on the priority list and begin to do the prevention to keep yourself healthy for the long term. Changing your diet takes time and dedication. But in order to live your best life you will need to get serious about your health and that includes your diet.

I absolutely believe in doctors, but I also believe that we must get to the root of our issues. For more ideas on living a healthy life, read my blog at www.purelifeclub.com. You will find great articles, resources, and events on living a healthy life.

This week start to make changes in your diet that will improve your health. What is your body showing you? What illnesses do you have that can be reversed by changing your lifestyle? What can you do right now to start eating better?

WEEK 10

Commit to meditation and pray

Taking time in the morning to pray and meditate will help you to stay balanced and focused throughout the day. You will also notice that you become more peaceful throughout the day. You may have to get up earlier than usual to complete this step. Start out with 15 minutes and then work your way up to a half hour. Sit in a quiet space and focus on scriptures or specific words such as *peace, love,* and *abundance.* I also like to focus on my breathing while meditating, enjoying each breath as I draw in air. It not only helps me to relax but it puts me in a gratitude state of mind. It's OK if you lose focus while meditating. It is a part of the learning process. The key is to refocus your attention when you drift off. Soon you will notice that it will become easier for you to stay calm and centered as you practice daily.

The basics of mindful meditation are as follows: Sit quietly in a yoga position on the floor or in a chair sitting upright. Begin to draw your breath in, allowing your stomach to become full like a balloon, and then slowly release the air, deflating the balloon. Take several deep breaths. Begin to focus on the words *peace, love,* or *joy.* Your mind may wander at first and that is OK. The Buddhists call this "the monkey mind." Bring your focus back to the breath. Holding your breath on the inhale is helpful staying focused. Continue with your breathing for several inhales and exhales. Allow yourself to feel free of judgment and experience the solace of peace.

Guided meditation CDs are a great way to start this practice. Many people find guided meditation to be instrumental in starting and maintaining their meditation practice. The key is to find a voice that you can easily follow.

Find a good class with a supportive teacher and peers. Many meditation classes are offered free or at a low cost. There are many forms of meditation, so go ahead and experiment with the different ones and find what resonates the best with you.

What did you notice about yourself? What thoughts and feelings arose during meditation?

Journal Notes

WEEK 11

Get moving

Yes take a walk or run, get in nature, and just notice the beauty of the Lord. It's amazing what the brain does when you move your body. There is much new research in the area of mind and body connection. And more evidence points to the correlation between exercising and intelligence. People who exercise regularly tend to have higher IQs than those who are sedentary. There is also evidence that exercising decreases the onset of Alzheimer's disease. So not only does exercise fight off disease but it also will make you smarter.

Incorporating regular exercise doesn't have to be difficult. The key is to plan ahead and schedule your exercise in for the week. Next you want to pack a gym bag with your basics such as running shoes. Now you are ready to go for a walk on your lunch break or in a park before you go home for the evening. I love group activities so I get my exercise by attending Zumba, Spin, or Yoga class.

How can you put regular exercise in your routine? What is holding you back from committing to a regular exercise program? Why do you neglect taking care of yourself? Is it only when we fully love ourselves that we can commit to a routine of taking care of ourselves?

WEEK 12
Get a massage

Treat yourself to a massage this week, and if you are already doing this, you have the go-ahead to get some extra spa treatments or relax at a spa for the weekend. If you're on a budget, that's OK. Massage therapy is within almost everyone's reach. There are many schools that train massage practitioners. As a part of training to be a massage therapist, many students offer free or low-cost massages.

A colleague shared with me that one of her secrets to looking so vibrant and young was her weekly massages. Tanya, well into her late forties, looked as though she was in her early thirties. She shared that she learned this tip from a mentor. Tanya credits massage for keeping her skin tight and her circulation flowing freely in her body.

Massage therapy is more than just a temporary feel-good session. It has been proven that physiological and psychological changes occur with regular therapeutic massage. Massage decreases anxiety, lowers blood pressure, induces sleep, improves concentration, diminishes aches and pains, and has many other wonderful benefits. The power of touch is an amazing tool that we all need. Go ahead and schedule a massage session today, knowing that you are helping your body and mind stay balanced and healthy.

How did you feel before and after the massage? Did you notice a decrease of tension? What are the benefits of making this ritual a regular part of your lifestyle?

Journal Notes

WEEK 13
Do a cleansing fast

Do a fruit and veggie fast to refresh and rejuvenate your body. The amazing thing about a fruit or veggie fast is that it wakes the body up. Many times people will report feeling clearer and more focused after a fast. A fast is a great way to jumpstart a healthy eating plan. In today's society we often eat many processed and high-sugar foods, which are not healthy and are highly addictive. Research has shown that sugar is just as addictive as crack cocaine. The brain constantly wants that chemical high to feel good and to maintain balance. Making the switch to healthy and nutritious food is not always easy as we fight off cravings. Breaking a food addiction is similar to going into detox for drugs or alcohol. You may experience withdrawal symptoms such as nausea, headaches, or cravings. However, the benefits of cleansing far outweigh the temporary side effects of clearing your body. Once you have completed your cleanse, you may notice that vegetables and fruits are more appealing to you. You may also notice that your food cravings have disappeared.

Not only is it important to prepare the foods you will eat on your fast, but you should also prepare emotionally. I like to use affirmations and scriptures that help to reaffirm what God says about my body and health. Keep a journal of how you feel throughout the process. Take walks to calm your spirit as your body detoxifies and repeat your scriptures throughout the day. Making fasting a part of a routine during the change of seasons or once a week will help to keep you mentally and physically healthy.

What did you notice about yourself during the fast? What food did you crave the most? Did you experience headaches? Were you cranky? Did you notice a boost in your energy level? Did your physical appearance improve? Did you experience a spiritual healing or renewal?

WEEK 14
Rest

Really just chill this week. Say no to everything!

Women are trained to give and oftentimes we give until it hurts. We often give our time and resources out of obligation and guilt. This week focus on giving out of love. Start by saying no to every request. Simply say, "Let me check my schedule and I will get back to you." Then process the request. Start by asking yourself questions, such as: Does this fall in line with your purpose or what you are focused on right now? Do you feel good about it? Is this something you have wanted to do? Will this take you away from other obligations or the rest you need right now? Asking these questions will help you decide if this is something you really want to do. Allowing the answers to be a guide for your true intentions will serve you well in making good decisions.

I was blessed to hear John Maxwell speak a few years ago at a Joyce Meyer Women's Conference. Mr. Maxwell stated that you can always turn a "No" into a "Yes" but it is difficult to turn a "Yes" into a "No." Since that time, I have made it a practice to say "No" first. This allows me time to think about and process the idea. This simple shift in my thinking has helped me to give to myself and others out of love rather than obligation.

Sometimes we need to shut down and just gather our thoughts. Some call this a mental health break. I simply call this a time of disconnection. As human beings, our bodies can become drained. Taking a break from all activities and just resting can help to restore our body and mind. During your mini break, resist answering emails, checking into social media networks, and talking to friends on the phone. Focus on calming the body and mind by reading a good book. Writing in your journal, gardening, yoga and walking outdoors help to restore and revitalize the spirit.

What did you notice about yourself during this time of resting and reflection? Did you feel more energized after your break? What did you gain from this experience and what will you incorporate into these resting periods in the future?

Journal Notes

4

Commitment

"There's a difference between interest and commitment. When you're interested in doing something, you do it only when circumstances permit. When you're committed to something, you accept no excuses, only results."

—ART TUROCK

Complete something

I don't care what it is, you need to finish some project that you started and never completed. Failure to complete it is not an option. Yes there are many things that you have left undone, but there are also many you have completed. Now pick up where you left off. Ask the Lord for inspiration and finish it. So many times we stop because we think well we are not famous who will notice. I can never be at the top so why bother. The answer to that is God knows. He has placed abundant talent in you. He has given you gifts and one day you will be held accountable for them. Encourage yourself, knowing that you are doing it for him. God delights in his children when he sees us using the gifts and talents he placed in us. So make a commitment to finish something.

Understand that resistance will rear its ugly head in the process of completing a task that is a part of your destiny. Have you ever tried to move forward on a personal goal and found that you were met with a lot of resistance? An example would be you have just decided to take better care of your health and to eat better. You are excited and motivated! Then you enter your workplace and someone offers you a donut. Better yet, Susie has a birthday and shares some cake. If you are unarmed with a response, you eat the donut and then later you have some cake. Before long you decide I'll start tomorrow.

Resistance comes in many forms. Last week I decided that I would walk every day outdoors and just enjoy what God gives us naturally, Mother

Nature. Then it rained all week! But I had a contingency plan. I would do a home video or go to the gym if the weather was not on my side.

Resistance can be someone or something that is opposing what you know that you need for yourself right now. I encourage you to embrace resistance because the more we push past the opposition the stronger we become. Resistance is a tool that allows us to know we are on the right track. What resistance have you met recently? What action will you take when others or things stand in your way? Do you have a contingency plan for life's distractions?

Write a list of projects that you would like to complete. Begin to list the projects according the approximate amount of time it would take to complete the project. For example, organizing your receipts may take one hour and completing a photo album may take two to four hours. What projects will you complete this week? How did it feel to finish a project that you started?

WEEK 16

Run a race

As I prepared for the race, I was excited about running my first race. This would be the first of many races that I would participate in with my middle daughter. My excitement and joy could not be denied as I hurried to the starting line. As I ran, there were cheerleaders on the sidelines who spurred us on. They would say to us, "You can do it; you're almost there." I was excited every time I saw them. Then it hit me I was not almost there, I still had 2.5 miles to go. But somehow the encouragement made me want to run even more. There were times during this run that I wanted to stop. But I remained committed to completing this event. As the terrain got tougher with hills I would think about quitting. But out of nowhere, I would hear a spectator shouting, "You are doing great and you're almost at the finish line." It was like they knew what I was thinking. It was in this moment that I realized how God will provide us encouragement along our journey if we just stay committed to completing the race.

Encouragement is very important as it propels us to surpass what we think we cannot do and what seems unattainable. All my life, I have been committed to encouraging others. Now someone was encouraging me. Every time we want to give up or stop, someone or a symbol will appear, urging us on. "You are almost there; keep going. You're almost at the finish line."

As you reflect on your life, can you recall a time when you overcame a difficult situation or surpassed what you thought you couldn't do? How were you guided to complete the race?

WEEK 17

Thank God for now!

Yes sit and be still and thank God for where
you are, even if you are not where you want
to be. Thank God you are not where you use to
be. If you are in the midst of a storm, thank God
for his mercy and grace to carry you through.
Thank him for basic needs such as food, shelter,
transportation, whatever it is. Thank God for
the extraordinary gifts that you have received. I
will never forget this one evening when I looked
up and saw the most perfect full moon. It was a
beautiful clear night. As I took a moment to just

be still and notice this miracle, I recall thinking we are so blessed to witness sights like this.

Meditation is a wonderful way to start being more present every day. While sitting quietly and upright, begin to meditate on thankfulness. Begin to breathe in and out. Recite in your mind: "I am thankful for now." "I am thankful for this present moment." "I am thankful for this breath." Allow yourself to breathe that in. Notice how you feel throughout your body. Notice what thoughts come up in your mind. Then return to the world grateful, thankful, and at peace. Take three slow breaths and reflect on the simple pleasures of life that are often overlooked. Throughout the day, you may simply observe nature and notice how it gives us life. Training our minds to be present and grounded in gratitude takes time but is a lesson worth investing in. Start this practice by taking five to 10 minutes each day to reflect on being present to the lessons of gratitude.

Sonja Lyubomirsky, the author of *The How of Happiness,* writes that gratitude is one of the keys to happiness. Being thankful increases our capacity to experience joy and love. Write a list of what you are thankful for right now. What are you blessed with? What lessons have you learned from your trials and achievements?

Journal
Notes

WEEK 18

Start journaling

S tart journaling to discover yourself again. Journaling allows you to express yourself through writing. It's such a powerful tool for connecting with your innermost thoughts. I started journaling when I was 14 years old. I recall watching an *Oprah Winfrey Show* where she discussed the power of journaling. Oprah encouraged everyone to keep a gratitude journal. (In Week 43, I will give you more details on creating a gratitude journal that will change your life.) What a powerful concept that I could choose to be grateful every day. It was in this moment that I realized that we always have something to be thankful for, even if it was just for our heart beating every second.

As a young adult, my family life was dysfunctional, to put it mildly, but I dreamed of having a future like Bill and Clair Huxtable from *The Cosby Show*. I believe that getting in touch with my emotions at such a young age really helped me to shape my future and to have that healthy family life that I craved as a child. No matter your age or circumstance, begin to write. Write about your day, hopes, dreams, or frustrations. Start your journal with a thank-you to God for this day. It will help to center you. I start my journal with "Dear God." That really guides me in the idea that God is always with me and ready to hear what is going on in my life.

Journaling can be a wonderful tool that can give you a sense of freedom. Write about your hopes, dreams, and disappointments. What are your goals? Who do you love? What do you love? Journal topics can range from thoughts of gratitude to what gave you joy today. Write about your dreams, disappointments, and your daily successes.

Journaling is fun, but it also helps to give you a roadmap for your journey. When I look back at old journals, I can see the growth that I have had. It's like looking back at a young me through my eyes. If you already journal, then that's wonderful. Try focusing your journal topics on themes such as "the 5 best things that happened to me today," "what I most enjoyed today," "who I blessed today," and "prayers answered today."

I love a new journal. I usually take weeks to pick out the perfect journal. Another one of my rituals is to write my yearly goals on my birthday in my journals. I prefer birthdays for setting goals rather than the traditional New Year's resolutions. What is special about your journals? How has journaling helped you? What time of day do you journal?

How will you start your journal? How will you incorporate journaling into your regular routine? First, start with the commitment to begin a journal this week.

Journal Notes

WEEK 19
Refrain from shopping

At least once a month, make a commitment to take a holiday from shopping. During your weekend, make good use of things that you already have. One of my favorite activities is to make a new recipe from ingredients that I already have. It allows me to realize how fortunate I am to have a cabinet full of food and a stove to cook it on. I also like to pull out old books and read them or rearrange the clothes in my closet. It still amazes me that I find new things every time!

Refraining from shopping will allow you to reflect on what you already have. It will help you to prioritize what is important in your life. This exercise will also help you to recognize how blessed you already are. Sometimes the act of doing nothing brings us self-awareness that allows us to understand our natural abundance and the tendency we have to go outside of ourselves for artificial satisfaction.

What did you discover during this time? Did you notice how blessed you already are? Did you suffer from shopping withdrawal? How can you instill this principle into the lives of your children?

WEEK 20

Develop a morning routine

Many years ago I discovered the power of an early morning. I would get up a couple of hours before everyone else. This quiet time allowed me time to reflect and prepare for the day. I have also used this time to write, go on walks and to organize various projects. I value this time and protect it by not taking phone calls or watching the morning news. Imagine how different your life could be if you had a few extra hours or even thirty minutes to peacefully work at something you enjoyed each day. You would probably have a happier and more productive day. Long lasting results requires a shift in our patterns.

Here are some simple ideas to implement so you can have productive and peaceful mornings:

1. Wake up a little earlier each morning. You'll need some extra time in the morning to accommodate your mindful changes. Going to bed earlier makes this task easier. Set your alarm for a half hour earlier each morning until you build up to an hour or 90 minutes.

2. Visualize and imagine good things. Right before you get out of bed, begin to imagine how well your day will go. Visualize yourself being productive, happy, and peaceful. I also like to use this time to meditate on the dreams that God has given me. Take some time to thank God for this new day that you will embark on.

3. Meditate. Take 10-20 minutes to practice meditation. Meditation brings awareness and focus and it allows us to get direct spiritual downloads. This will allow your day to have a peaceful glow to it.

4. Enjoy a little exercise. Take a walk, jump on the treadmill, or dance to some beautiful music. Focus on positive thoughts and get your body moving.

5. Shower yourself with affirmations. While taking your morning shower, repeat affirmations to yourself. Use this time to shower yourself with positive thoughts and energy. Affirmations can truly transform your thinking and your life.

6. Eat a nutritious breakfast. Having a green smoothie, vegetable omelet, or oatmeal with fruit will get you off to a great start. It is amazing how we feel when we take care of ourselves. Soon you will notice that you make better eating choices throughout the day. During your meal, take time to be mindful of the flavors, colors, smells, and

textures of your food. This practice of being mindful will add to your eating experience.

7. Drink a glass of water. Keep water by your bed and in your car. Drinking water the first thing in the morning compels your body to function at its optimal best. Drinking water keeps your body and mind hydrated. Yes your brain needs water to function at its optimal best. So drink up.

8. Write out and review your agenda for the day. Writing a list of priorities will assist you in making good decisions with your time throughout the day. Placing the most difficult task at the top of your list will help you to prioritize your daily tasks. Having a daily agenda will empower you to be more productive each day.

Now you're ready to get out there and accomplish something. What can you do to improve your morning routine? How has changing your morning routine impacted the flow of your day?

WEEK 21

Practice listening

Oftentimes we talk over other people or we are so excited about what is happening in our life that we don't really listen to others with our full attention. We all have been guilty of this at one time or another.

As we listen to others, we will become more fully aware of their needs and desires. We will also learn how we can best support them in their journey. This week make a commitment to listening to your partner, friend, and/or children.

Being a good listener takes practice and time, but with diligence, you and your loved ones will reap the benefits.

Here are few steps to being a good listener. Clear your mind of your agenda when listening to someone. Reflect back on what the person stated so you are clear as to what they wanted to communicate. Sometimes we wrongly interpret a person's body language when we are communicating. You can ask what it means. For example, "I notice you are shaking when you talk about your parents—what is going on?" The person may state they are worried or frustrated. Finally, before offering a solution or dismissing a person's feelings, ask them how you can support them right now. Many times we already have the answer but we just want to be understood and feel an emotional connection with the other person. Receiving empathy rather than a solution allows us to feel heard and understood.

What did you learn by listening to others? Did you find it hard not to interrupt? Did you notice how the flow of the conversation became different? Were you uncomfortable with the quiet peaks in the conversation?

Journal
Notes

5

Connection

"We need old friends to help us grow old
and new friends to help us stay young."

—LETTY COTTIN POGREBIN

Create the relationship you desire

A s a life coach and counselor, I am often asked, "How do I find the right person?" The answer is simpler than you may think. Love like any other emotion can be drawn to us by our output of emotions. You have the ability to turn up your love frequency and allow the Universe to draw your perfect mate to you. Over the years, I have witnessed countless friends, associates, and clients have divine connections after learning these principles. It is quite amazing how easily we connect with others when we are taking care of ourselves and giving service to others.

Relationship boards have had a great impact on my life. You really can have the love you desire. Here are 7 keys that will get you there.

1. Create a vision board that focuses on positive relationships and the attributes you most desire in a mate. You may place gifts, words of affirmation, or services on them. Place pictures of places you would like to travel to together or fun hangouts. Add words to your board that have value to you such as *commitment, compromise, laughter, romance, security, family-oriented,* and *free spirit.* Remember to focus on what you truly desire in a mate and not what your mom or friends may want for you. Being authentic is key to building a great board that will work for you.

2. Imagine what life would be like with your new mate. Begin to smell the warm scents of evenings snuggled up on the sofa in front of the fireplace or the salty aroma as you walk hand in hand along the beach. Imagine the laughter and the fun you will have together. Think of a tough situation and imagine your new partner giving you the support you desire. Maybe your new partner will hold your hand and just listen to you as you express your thoughts. Taking time to just imagine life with your soul mate will allow you to instinctively know the qualities you desire in a partner and will help you kiss the frogs and move on quickly until you have hit that sweet spot.

3. Create affirmations that affirm your best qualities. Repeat them daily. Also create a set of affirmations that relate to the relationship you desire. For example: "My mate adores me." "I am pleasantly surprised by my mate." "My soul mate is drawn to me." Affirmations are strong because they speak to the Universe your desires. The Universe

has no choice but to deliver to you what you believe is true.

4. Mind your words. Just as affirmations have the power to deliver what we desire so do the negative words we speak. If you are constantly saying "nobody wants me" or "all the men are taken," you are affirming your beliefs in the negative. Guess what, you will continue to get what you speak. According to Proverbs 18:21, our words have the power of life and death. So speak life-affirming words and soon you will have the happy and healthy relationship you desire.

5. The Universe wants to meet your needs but you are required to take action. Your soul mate wants to meet you now. So this is big! When you are invited to a party or asked to an event by someone new such as a business colleague or work buddy, go! It is just that simple. Oftentimes we refuse new ideas and go with the same old thing that we are accustomed to. Divine connections are waiting to happen every day so make today your day.

6. Keep your heart grounded in gratitude. Begin to be joyful for the life you have already. Embrace the pleasant moments that occur on a day-to-day basis. The more you are grateful for the life you have created, the more someone else will want to join you in your joy. If you are currently experiencing a sad unlived life, pump it up. Begin to do things that place you in a happy state.

7. Be very clear about who you are and what you bring to the table. Many times we believe we have to change ourselves to meet our perfect mate. The truth is once you have made certain changes you are no longer authentic. Self-improvement is great, but be sure to make authentic changes that you desire, not ones you think others will appreciate. Changes that are not true are hard to maintain and eventually will be disappointing to someone who believed that was who you were. Take time to highlight your best qualities. If you love to cook then practice preparing great meals for your mate. If you love traveling then travel with the idea that one day you will share your travel

journeys with your mate. Take this alone time to develop your true self and to enjoy life. Go ahead and *live*!

I love to hear great love stories. Please write me at Melisa@MelisaAlaba.com and let me know how this book inspired you, led you to your soul mate, or helped you overcome an untrue belief.

Journal Notes

Create a new tradition

I truly value holiday traditions. Growing up we didn't have many traditions, so I was intentional about having special holiday traditions in my household. This was great for me and my kids, but I also noticed that old traditions can sometimes be limiting. For example, it had become routine to have Christmas dinner at my home. This of course means we cannot go out of town or to someone's home for Christmas dinner.

Recently, we traveled to a cabin in the mountains of Ellijay, Georgia, for Christmas. This was one of the best Christmases that I ever experienced. As a family, we had an opportunity to bond over games, campfires, and walking on the trails. The holiday became about celebrating each other rather than about the presents under the tree or preparing for visitors. Another unexpected reward of that holiday was that everyone got to rest. We all pulled out our favorite books and just enjoyed some quiet time without all the distractions of our busy world.

A simple change of traditions can help you to gain new perspectives and allow you time to wonder about new possibilities in your life. We decided as a family that we liked this tradition of a traveling holiday so much that we would incorporate it every other year.

How do you spend special holidays? What changes would you like to make? Or how can you incorporate new traditions into your family life?

Journal Notes

WEEK 24

Plan a girlfriend's night out

Plan a girl's night out. At least once a month get together to do something new. One of my friends recently had a painting party. Everyone came and discussed their hopes and dreams while they worked on their portraits over food and companionship. Many of my friends plan parties around their favorite hobbies or interests.

It is important that we take time to cherish the people that we love. Experiencing events together, whether they are out on the town or dinner at home, allows us to stay connected to one another. Our joyful memories keep us grounded in our relationships. So many times we support each other through hardship, which is important, but it is equally important to share fun times together. During good times, we learn more about the likes and dislikes of our friends in a calm and peaceful environment. This draws us closer together when we need encouragement from each other.

What event can you plan? If you are wondering about new things in your area, sign up for livingsocial.com or groupon.com. Many local businesses provide excellent deals on these sites. You will receive alerts to different events and specials in your area. The growth that we experience when we try new things is amazing.

This week select and do something new with your girlfriends. How did this exercise empower and inspire you? What will you try next?

Journal Notes

WEEK 25

Join a new networking group

Before my cross-country move to Atlanta, I had a few good friends, but I always wanted a set of friends that shared my love for business. I wanted to hang out with some innovative women who could empower me to grow. My move forced me to expand my network of friends. However, you do not need to move out of state to cultivate new relationships. You can meet people through social media sites such as Facebook or Meetup.com.

One day while looking for office space, I met a witty tech geek, Lisa Richardson, who invited me to a Facebook group. Soon I discovered what I had longed for—a group of smart, funny businesswomen. We not only hung out in a Facebook forum, we also supported each other's businesses at events and workshops. I am so grateful for the experience of having this supportive network. The Atlanta Women's Business Group helped me to reclaim my power in a new place.

I also found that the online Meetup.com Forums introduced me to many new people who shared my interests and hobbies. After attending a golf clinic through Meetup.com, I was hooked. I soon started the Pure Life Club using the Meetup.com site for organizing the event. The group immediately attracted members who wanted to learn meditation and lead a holistic life style. Our members are encouraged and inspired by continuing their practice with new people. Connecting with new people each month at this Meetup group has been a beautiful experience.

What are some of your hobbies or interests that you would like to share with others? How can you develop a group around that idea? How can having a supportive network help you on your path? Commit to meeting new people who share your interests each month.

Journal Notes

WEEK 26

Hug someone

Touch is so powerful. It gives our body this instant release of endorphins and raises our awareness. Sometimes all it takes is a hug to encourage somebody.

A few years ago, I experienced such a moment. At my annual women's retreat, we were instructed to hug our neighbor. So everyone started embracing each other. The energy was amazing. We then were instructed to hug another person. I reached out and hugged the woman to my right. As I embraced her, she pulled back and said, "OK that's enough" and "I am not a hugger." Because I knew the emotion of touch was so powerful, I instinctively knew this woman had been wounded. Later, she stated that in that hug moment she experienced pain as old issues from the past resurfaced. She later shared that she knew it was time to heal those old scars so she could be free to experience touch in a positive manner.

Touch is powerful and many times we ignore its impact. A lack of touch will cause a person to become sick, angry, and coldhearted. Touch gives us a feeling of connection and being loved. Many times a marriage therapist will prescribe touch therapy to couples who have relationships that lack intimacy. Regular loving touch promotes intimacy, relationship, and better communication. So go ahead and hug somebody today. How do you show love to your children, family members, and spouse? Did you grow up in a household where physical affection was a normal occurrence? How has that affected your interactions with others?

Journal
Notes

WEEK 27

Get your hair wet

So much of our journey involves taking a risk and choosing to participate in life. Yet when the opportunity comes to play our life out loud we balk. So I invite you to get your hair wet. The next time you are invited to go rafting, try hot yoga, or join in on a new activity, just do it.

Forget about what your hair will look like. Disregard your desire to compare yourself to others in the class or at the activity and just join in. Take this time to be yourself. Being authentic is a process. The process requires that we let go of our self-doubts and judgments and learn to be comfortable in every situation.

One of the biggest reasons I often hear from my clients for not trying something new is they fear getting their hair wet. Wet hair is a symbol for being vulnerable and open. When your hair is wet, you can no longer hide behind the style or pretend you have it all together. You are forced to be goofy and silly and to live in the moment.

I challenge you to be purposeful in finding an activity that requires you to get your hair wet. What activity will you participate in? How did you feel with your hair wet?

6

Discovery

"*When we free ourselves from the constraints of ordinary goals and uninformed scoffers, we will find ourselves roaring off the face of the earth.*"

—ABRAHAM MASLOW

WEEK 28
Create a blog

For many people, writing a blog is a liberating experience. A blog can be an online journal that chronicles your life, interests, or events that you attend. A blog allows you to share your knowledge, thoughts, and ideas with others via the Internet. I started a blog in 2009. I found it helped me to express myself. Over the years, my blog has shifted from my innermost thoughts to words of wisdom on living a holistic life. You can create a blog around things that interest you also. I have had the opportunity to follow and meet bloggers who are making a powerful impact in our community. Vernetta Freeney, Stacey Ferguson, and Crystal Collins are bloggers who I follow and respect for their online and offline contributions.

While on Facebook, I met Vernetta Freeney. She is the founder of Women Are Game Changers. We immediately bonded through Facebook and promised to meet face-to-face one day. While she was in the Atlanta area on business, Vernetta and I sat down for a chat, which lasted for hours. She is truly a force to be reckoned with. She is a former educator that turned her passion for writing into a profitable career. She specializes in helping women build their networking skills, business etiquette, and true fashion style.

At an award program, I was honored to meet Stacy Ferguson, a blogger who developed a mommy blog. She and several of her friends chronicled their experience as working mothers. Soon the mommy blogs began to inspire women across the nation. Since that time, Stacy and her co-bloggers have formed Blogalicious to help other bloggers stay encouraged as they develop their blog and build a following. Blogging is fun, and it also can help you develop your purpose and create an additional income.

Lastly I can't forget Crystal Collins, who is a life style blogger. Crystal has become an authority on eating and living healthy on a budget. The Natural Thrifty blog offers ideas and products that will help you live your optimal life. She has turned her passion for creating natural health information into multiple blogs that bring in the advertising dollars for her family. So what are you waiting for? Create your blog today. Success will only come to those willing to do the work.

What will you write about? What interest would you like to develop? How has blogging helped you discover your purpose?

Journal Notes

Take an online class or attend a lecture series

Have you ever said to yourself, "I would love to learn about writing or how to sew," but over time you allowed yourself multiple excuses such as I don't have enough time or the financial resources to do it. Decide today to be a lifelong learner. All that is required is the mindset that you can learn something new every day. Many colleges, businesses, and online learning programs offer courses on various topics. So what are you itching to learn? What have you always craved to know more about?

Over the years, I have had the privilege of taking business courses, sewing classes, wine tasting classes, and a lecture course from Harvard. Learning something new will help to keep you creative, alive, and interesting.

Here are a few online sources that offer classes for free. Dive in and start today.

- The University of Hawaii sponsors a free eight-week course on Mindfulness Meditation. This course is interactive and is presented by Dr. Thanh V. Huynh. sites.google.com/site/ mindfulnessonlinecourse/
- Academic Earth and Open Learn both offer free courses from many of the universities across the nation. You can contact Academic Earth at academicearth.org/universities and Open Learn at open.edu/openlearn

- The Annenberg Foundation offers a variety of educational videos on various topics from math to psychology. This library is fitting for grade school to college level students. You can access this library at learner.org
- The Massachusetts Institute of Technology (MIT) offers lecture series on multiple subjects at ocw.mit.edu

What did you discover about yourself through this process? What other courses would you like to take in the future? How will you incorporate learning into your lifestyle?

Journal Notes

WEEK 30

Bake something

Go ahead and free your inner Sunny Anderson, renowned chef. It is so wondrous—the beauty that comes from creating a sweet dish— the joy that arises as your senses come alive to the sweet aroma of something baking in the oven. Over the years, I have embraced baking. Baking has created this great bond between me and my daughters. We enjoy experimenting with new flavors and spices. They have developed a keen sense of taste because of it. One of the great lessons that has come from our time in the kitchen is that we all have learned to embrace our personal power to create something special.

One game that the girls and I played was doing a bakeoff with the ingredients in our pantry and refrigerator. We would use the odds and ends that were already in the house to come up with something new. Each person was challenged to come up with the tastiest recipe. My husband always seemed to lose this one. I recall a smoothie challenge. He decided to make a plantain and coconut smoothie. Needless to say, it did not turn out so well. But we all had so much fun in the kitchen and a very good laugh.

Learn, enjoy, and create no matter where you are in life. Use what you have to make lemons into lemon squares or old bread into bread pudding.

What new recipe did you create? Did you turn an old family recipe into a healthy recipe? Did you discover a new family favorite?

Journal
Notes

WEEK 31
Make a must-do list

Write a list of all the things that you want
to do but never seem to have enough time
to do. For example, you may have always wanted
to take a yoga or tai chi class. Maybe you would
like to organize your family pictures or read a
book that a friend recommended. Each week
pick *one thing* that you will try. Changing your
weekly routines will awake you from the inside
and allow creativity to flow. Keep your must-do
list visible at work and at home so when you
have some spare time you can just do it. Creating

a must-do list really helped me when I was feeling particularly stuck one weekend. I was home alone with my baby and she required so much of my attention it was hard to focus for very long on anything else.

I decided to go to a local bookstore and just skim over a book I wanted to read but had no time for at that moment. I soon realized that just the act of moving toward my goal boosted my creativity and lifted my spirit. Scientists have discovered that the mere act of window shopping, skimming items online, or writing down our desires lifts our mood and makes us feel happier and abundant in our present state.

My list was a reminder of things I would soon return to. It also reminded me to just be still and enjoy my present moment because it too was fading. At the time of this writing, my youngest child is two and half years old. My life has mostly gotten back to normal. She is potty training and talking in sentences. As I look at her, I am reminded that she will never be a baby again.

I can now enjoy things on my list, such as hot yoga on Sunday afternoons, long walks in the park, and hiking in the woods. Life is a wonderful evolution that continues to flow as we grow. It's our job to grab hold of the branches and follow the flow.

What have you longed to do but have not done? Did you notice a shift in your thinking when you wrote down your must-do list? Did you feel that you had lived a little more each week because you tried something new or accomplished something on your list?

Journal Notes

WEEK 32

Go to the conference

I love getting out, and whenever I have an opportunity to attend a seminar or conference, I go. I am astounded by the creativity that flows from my being during and after attending one of these events. The pure energy of the crowd helps to open up windows of possibility within us. Tony Robbins, a well-known self-help author and motivational speaker, recently said that we draw from the energy banks of each other during such events. I am sure this is why many of his attendees walk the bed of fire after one of his events.

They feel like they can do anything and open themselves up to new possibilities.

When I attend conferences, I am like a kid in a candy story. I feel myself growing as I hear from others who have traveled the road I am going on and have landed on the other side. In order to be a good leader or teacher, we must first learn to follow. It takes a lot of energy, creativity, and efficiency to put together an event. I am often reminded of how creative we are as humans to be able to collaborate and organize on such a high level.

Additionally, our minds are able to reflect and assimilate during adult learning activities. We often find that we have "aha moments" that we can use in our personal and professional life. I have also been very fortunate to have met some wonderful people during these events who share many of my values, goals, and beliefs. In order to raise the level of our connections and our life, we must take ourselves to higher peaks. It is so important to nurture your spirit when you are moving to the next phase of your life. Attending empowering conferences and events can help you in fulfilling your goals.

This week plan to attend a conference, workshop, or lecture sometime this month.What did you learn? How did you feel? Did you notice a shift in your thinking? How can you continue to apply this principle to your life?

Journal Notes

WEEK 33

Get naked

Growing up I had come to hate my body. I remember as a child my cousin walked in on me in the bathroom. Later he made an insulting remark about my stomach. This is when my body issues started. I began to feel ashamed of my curves and hide my body behind clothing. I never allowed myself to be naked in front of others. Not even in a locker room or in front of my husband.

In order to change this belief and to get to self-love, I needed to let go. But how? I challenged myself to get naked in front of others. But after years of feeling unattractive I had to ease into this exercise. Here are a few things I did and some tips that will help you also.

I began to follow a beautiful blog called See Body. Love Self. On this blog, Ivy LaArtista writes about self-love and challenges us to embrace all of our flaws and imperfections. Ultimately self-love comes when we accept all of us. Each day I implemented small steps to meet my challenge. I started slowly undressing in the hallway of my home rather than rushing into the bathroom. I begin to experiment with being nude around my house.

Then I took the ultimate plunge. I visited JeJu Sauna in Duluth, Georgia. Modeled after a traditional Korean bathing house, JeJu offers steam baths and saunas, with many services requiring nudity. It was an uplifting, liberating and enlightening experience. I felt the love of God surrounding me. I enjoyed a body scrub, hip bath, and all the steam rooms. I prayed and meditated as I gently and fully let go of my hang-up of being nude in front of others. It was amazing to me how women bonded with each other as we took in the serenity of the quiet warmth of the spa.

How have body issues held you back? What will you do to let go of a negative self-image? What do you love the most about your body?

WEEK 34

Go organic!

Every day we encounter someone who truly believes in using organic products or eating organic foods. Many organic products and foods offer us an opportunity to reduce the chemicals that we place in and on our bodies and in our homes. Many of the ailments that we suffer from can be eliminated by changing our habits. The idea of changing our lifestyle or altering our shopping habits may be overwhelming at first. So start with the basics.

A simple way to start this is to add organic products mindfully starting with your head.

- MONTH 1: Switch your traditional hair care products with organic or homemade options. Many traditional products have sulfates in them that can cause damage to your hair and body.
- MONTH 2: Experiment with cooking foods with fresh organic vegetables. They have been shown to have the most nutritional value. Check out www.naturalthrifty.com for some wonderful ideas on eating well on whole foods.
- MONTH 3: Focus on your environment. Begin to substitute your cleaning supplies with more organic products.
- MONTH 4: Let's go wine tasting. Organic wines contain a lower amount of sulfites that may reduce headaches and drowsiness when consuming wine. Red wine has been shown to have many health benefits especially for the heart. Organic

wines come in a wide variety and are
offered at your local health food stores.

~ MONTH 5: We are on a roll. This month
try organic lotions and deodorant.
It's been found that aluminum, dyes,
and other toxic chemicals in the
lotions and deodorants that we use
every day may be harmful to your
health. Discover one of my favorite
organic soaps, Oatmeal almond, at
www.thegreenyoniboutique.org.

Each month, continue to add things and activities to your lifestyle that make you feel good and that will allow you to live a long and healthy life.

One of the things you will begin to notice as you upgrade your living is that you will feel better. What changes have you noticed since you made the switch? What are your new favorite products?

Journal Notes

7

Forgiveness

"Be not the slave of your own past. Plunge
into the sublime seas, dive deep and swim
far, so you shall come back with self-respect,
with new power, with an advanced experience
that shall explain and overlook the old."

—RALPH WALDO EMERSON

Forgiveness is a beautiful act of letting go. I truly believe when we release pain, anger, bitterness, and regret we allow ourselves to enjoy a beautiful freedom.

Friend or foe?

Sometimes we have toxic relationships that continue to put us in an unhealthy place in our life. We deserve to be in good relationships that nurture our beings. Our relationships speak volumes about where we are mentally and physically. Oftentimes we emulate what we see our friends doing. When we have friends who are health conscious, we tend to eat better around them. Likewise if we have friends who gossip or speak negatively of themselves or others we tend to follow that behavior. Now if you are one of those people who are not affected by the negative folks in your life that is commendable. But it is also a daunting task to have to constantly defend your beliefs in your inner circle. To begin the process of creating a sisterhood of positive and uplifting sisters, start by clearing out the bad relationships in your life. You may also want to explore what type of a friend you are as well.

After you clear yourself of unhealthy relationships, you are in a position to cultivate new relationships. Ask God to send good people in your life that can walk with you on your journey of living your best life. As we age, it becomes harder to connect with new people on a deeper level. So set out to be purposeful in building new relationships. Talk to people, other women or men, who inspire you at work or in groups that you participate in. Ask them out to breakfast or lunch. You will be surprised at how quickly you build new relationships when you begin to make an effort in this area.

Begin to cultivate relationships that support you in your dreams, goals, and aspirations.

Having a buddy system supporting you in good health, positivity, and spirituality is wonderful and will support you on your transformation into being a better person. Do your current friendships support the person you long to be? What attributes do you offer your friends?

WEEK 36

Encourage yourself—you can do it!

Sometimes you feel like who listens to me. But be of good cheer, learn to encourage yourself. It may feel like the whole world is against you, that you have done your best but nothing seems to be moving in the right direction. Well, I have been there. I recall sitting down teary-eyed and just wishing there was someone I could reach out to—someone who could understand my trials and tribulations. What I found is that most times the people closest to us during our time of need are not available emotionally to give us the support we long for. In fact, the very person we want to help us may have an issue as well. So I have learned to encourage myself.

Yes it can be tough at times, but I remember that God loves me, and as Psalm 138:8 says, "He has a good plan for my life." This uplifts my spirit and keeps me headed toward the prize. So forgive yourself, encourage yourself, and move forward.

When you find you are in a tough situation, encourage yourself. Bring to your memory times when God has seen you through. Recall and state out loud the victories that you have had over your life time. What have you overcome? How has God shown favor in your life? Start to express gratitude for the many blessings that you have. Soon you will feel the victor rise up on the inside of you. Remembering the good things can be of great encouragement as we move forward. Every situation is temporary but our spiritual connection is eternal. Learning to encourage yourself is a great gift because you can use it when no one is around.

What scriptures or words of encouragement can you use to bring you through a tough situation or just a bad day?

WEEK 37

Get rid of loose skin

Many extremely overweight individuals have loose skin after they experience a dramatic weight loss. The skin serves as a reminder of their struggles and the pain they once held. Doctors generally advise them to have reconstructive surgery to remove the extra skin. This serves two purposes: one to improve their self-esteem and two to improve their physical health, because loose skin can cause infections if not cleaned properly. Past trauma in our lives such as divorce and loss of a job, home, or loved one can be like loose skin. We often carry around unwanted reminders of that period in our life. Although those situations may have brought us joy at one point in our lives, now the remnants bring up pain. Pain can be in the form of bitterness, anger, resentment, blame, or mistrust. And often we begin to carry this baggage around with us.

Choose to forgive daily. Jesus said we should forgive our neighbor 77 times per day (Matthew 18:22). Wow, that's a lot of forgiving. I believe his point was that we all are imperfect and we need to understand one another's flaws. It's not always the big things that keep us from forgiving each other. Ever notice how small issues can build up to resentment over time? I have seen so many marriages fail over small things. This week practice letting go of any anger you have daily.

Think of your loved one as someone you want to cherish for a lifetime with all their imperfections and quirks. Choose to focus on the good that they bring into your life. Soon you will realize that the small things really aren't as important as we make them in the moment. I encourage you to have the surgery and get rid of the loose skin today.

What emotions or physical reminders are you holding on to that need to be let go? Write a list of everything that you need to let go of. It is time to give it all back to God. You no longer need to carry the pain. The Lord has set you free. So accept your deliverance and let it go. Practice letting go of old issues, regrets or hurts during morning meditation. What did you discover about yourself? Were you holding on to things that you thought you had let go many years ago? While reflecting on your list, were you able to see how holding on has affected the joy and peace in your life?

Journal Notes

WEEK 38

Write your life story: beginning, middle, and end

Begin to write your story. List the names of each chapter. What would you change? If you don't like the story, change it. It's your story; how do you want to end it? When we are stuck or in a rut, it is hard for us to envision anything different. But we have to understand that all situations are temporary, nothing lasts forever in its present state. With that knowledge, we can apply new thoughts to our life. Instead of living in anger and disappointment, we can acknowledge the source of these feelings and let them go. We can forgive others and forgive ourselves.

Maybe you want to experience more joy or passion in your life. Allow yourself time to start imagining what that would feel like. How will the actions you take today affect your life story over time? You may notice that there are many areas that you are proud of in your story. Take this time to be grateful for the good moments that you have had.

I am most proud of how I have raised my daughters. When I think of all the time I spend with my daughters, I am pleased to know that when they are older they will have the satisfaction of knowing that they were cared for.

Think about your life on a whole. What are you doing right now that will leave an impact on this world that you cannot yet see? Do you feel encouraged to know that time will allow every small thing to be insignificant while the big things, such as spending time with our families, living a life of purpose, giving to others, and taking care of ourselves, will be magnified in the end?

What will your story look like? How did this exercise change your views of your life? How do you want to alter your story?

Journal Notes

8

Giving

"Do not withhold good from those who deserve it, when it is in your power to act."

PROVERB 3:27

I t is in our giving that we truly learn to trust God. I believe that when we give to others we experience the blessing of emulating our creator.

Giving is a divine expression that affords us the opportunity to develop trust with God. Each time we give, we speak to his heart by saying "I trust you will take care of me." We give because we know we have more than enough.

WEEK 39

Help somebody else meet their goals

This week pick someone that you would like to help with their business or life goals. If they are trying to lose weight, encourage them by offering to exercise with them or bring a healthy snack when you meet. If you have a friend who has recently started a business, you can encourage her by offering her an encouraging word or refer her to a new client. When we help others accomplish their dreams, God will send others to assist us in fulfilling our dreams.

You can choose to help someone in your family, at work, or in your neighborhood. I encourage you to decide to bless someone today. Maybe it's a mother in your community or a teenager who is struggling in your area. Instead of thinking of it as someone else's problem, commit to being a part of that person's journey. When we start to recognize that our purpose is connected to each other, it becomes easier to help others. God has shown me much favor and I know it is because I never forget those I love.

Who blessed you along the way? How has it impacted your life? How did it feel to help someone with their goals? How will you continue to incorporate this into your life?

Organize a fundraiser: Giving feels good

In Week 49 I tell how I put together a clothing drive at my daughter's school. I have also had the opportunity to organize fundraisers for women and other issues that I care about. There is something special about bringing people together for a common purpose that allows you to see how working together can produce great results.

One of my collogues, Sky Banks, has decided to be a champion for human immunodeficiency virus (HIV). She leads many fundraisers for the cause. She believes that by raising funds for this important cause she is raising awareness of the affect of HIV on African-American women. It is so amazing to see her at one of her events. The passion she has for prevention and early detection of HIV inspires you to want to give to her organization.

Ponder over what issues are important to you. How will you impact this world by dedicating your time as an organizer, chairperson, or fundraiser? You can even impact a cause by using your knowledge and connections to educate the community about the importance of your organization.

What issues are important to you? How can you help to create positive change in your community or internationally? Name several organizations for which you would like to organize a fundraiser. Then start putting together a team of other like-minded people to make it happen.

How did it feel to organize an event for your cause? What inspiration did you get from working with others?

WEEK 41

Give it away

I challenge you to give anonymously this week. When we give from a secret place we leave the expectation of a reward or reciprocation totally up to God because the recipient cannot return the favor. Go in your closet, office, or garage and pull out all the items you have in good condition that you have not used in the last year. Gather those items that you know someone would appreciate. Make a plan to donate them to an organization or give them to an individual who could use them.

Surprise a postal worker, daycare provider or maintenance person. You might leave an anonymous cash amount for a mom who uses public transportation. Instruct her with a note stating, " God loves you and you deserve to take a taxi today". Imagine her surprise when she receives it. Get creative in this give away.

The late Mary Kay Ash would often say you can never out give God. This is so true. Every time I give someone something out of love and kindness, I am amazed how God gives back to me tenfold. Over the summer, I decided to surprise a special young person with a laptop. He wanted to start a business and needed a computer to get him started. I am happy to announce that he started a tutoring company in his neighborhood and is ready to take on new ventures. I really believed in his dream so I invested in him.

At the time, my eldest daughter also desired a laptop but I felt she could wait for a while and share mine until I could buy her one. To my surprise, she was blessed with a brand-new Apple MacBook computer a few months later. She received the perfect computer to allow her to invest in her creative talents as a young director and producer. The computer was ten times the cost of the one I had purchased for the young man. You can never out give God. He will always meet your needs.

When we take time to bless others, we put ourselves in line to be blessed.

Who can you bless today? What treasures are you holding on to that someone can use right now? How have you been blessed by giving to others?

Journal Notes

9

Gratitude

"Gratitude unlocks the fullness of life. It turns what we have into enough, and more. It turns denial into acceptance, chaos to order, confusion to clarity. It can turn a meal into a feast, a house into a home, a stranger into a friend. Gratitude makes sense of our past, brings peace for today, and creates a vision for tomorrow."

—MELODY BEATTIE

There's something wonderful that happens when we express our gratitude. For me it's like a light just shines through to my soul. I am so appreciative of every wanted or unwanted gift granted to me. Gifts can come in all forms. They may come to you wrapped in an unpleasant experience or packaged beautifully in a box. Each day take a moment to say thank you for every breath because it truly is a gift.

WEEK 42

Write a thank-you letter

This week write a letter to somebody who has impacted your life. It may be someone who hurt you or taught you a life lesson. You may choose not to mail the letter. But just writing it will provide a release of love and forgiveness that is needed to move your life forward. Every experience that we have encountered over the years has led us to be the person we are today. Take time to acknowledge your appreciation for their love and generosity to you. It will bless them and release good in your life as well. If the lessons and gratitude were granted from a painful experience you may thank them for the lessons they have taught you about your own humanity. Allow this experience to provide you an opportunity to heal and grow as an individual.

When I think of my life, I know the catalyst for my path as a healer and coach was born through difficult situations. My ability to embrace those situations has allowed me to reach and teach others. I am truly thankful for everyone who abandoned or hurt me. I am equally grateful to those who supported and nurtured me. Life is a beautiful balance and when we learn to be thankful for the good and the not so good we move closer to our destiny. Rejoice in the lessons learned and embrace thankfulness.

Who has inspired you? What lessons have they taught you? How did writing a thank-you letter change your perspective?

WEEK 43

Start a
gratitude journal

We all have days that look impossible. I certainly have experienced that feeling. Everything seems to be going wrong. We think to ourselves that we will never accomplish our goals and receive the desires of our heart. We go through our day grumbling about what should and could have been.

These are the moments when we must dig deep in our soul and become thankful for all that is around us. If you don't have a house, then be thankful for your apartment. If you are living with someone else, be thankful for the space you have in their home. Be thankful for a bed. Be thankful for the grass and the flowers. Be thankful for your body being in motion. Be thankful that you can speak. Be thankful for a new day. Be thankful for your parents. Be thankful for your children. Be thankful to be married. Be thankful to be single. Be thankful if you are fat and be thankful if you are skinny.

Just be thankful for whatever you have right now because in the quiet moments of pure gratitude blessings abound. God wants to bless a thankful child. The more you are thankful for where you are right now, the more God is able to move in your life.

Journaling is a wonderful outlet to write about our highs and lows of the day. A gratitude journal focuses on the good that is happening in our life right now. I encourage you to start a gratitude journal. Each day record all the things that you are thankful for. Write about people, situations, or moments throughout the day that you felt blessed with or thankful for.

I find delight in recording small moments. Have you ever received an unexpected phone call in the middle of the day that made you smile from ear to ear? Recording these precious and happy moments reminds us that God is working every day—we just have to pay attention. Did you get a parking spot right in front of the store? Did a co-worker greet you with coffee? Record these special moments in your gratitude journal. I keep two journals: one in which I record my thoughts of the day and my gratitude journal. Over the years, my gratitude journal has become my favorite journal.

Writing regularly in your gratitude journal allows you to remember the resources you have now. We are so blessed because we have all we need right now to help us and to guide us in living a joyful life. No matter where you are on the economic scale, you have all it takes right in this moment to do what God has called you to do. Throughout the day, when you feel compelled to complain about someone or something, be reminded of what you are grateful for. Then speak words of gratitude.

As an added bonus, add gratitude affirmations to your journal. Speaking words of gratitude daily will encourage you and keep you in a thankful mindset. Here are a few examples:

- Thank you God for this beautiful day!
- Thank you God for supporting me in all my endeavors.
- I receive the love of the Universe today.
- I am loved.
- I am thankful for this moment.
- I am thankful for this breath.
- The beauty of the planet is amazing.
- I have more than enough.
- God is so good to me.
- I am a creator because my father is a creator.
- I am blessed by the very best.

Amen!

Journal Notes

10

Organization

"But all things should be done
decently and in order."

1 Corinthians 14:40

WEEK 44
Develop your brand

This week think of your personal brand. What does your image say about you? Our image often reflects the circumstances of our life. Ever notice how sick people look sick? Often we reveal ourselves through how we dress, our grooming, or take care of our health. Take a moment and ponder these questions: "If I were a name brand such as Nike, what would my slogan be? What does my image represent to the world?" While researching ideas for my company, I thought of this very thing. What do people think of when they meet me? My slogan is "Empowering you to live your best life." Do I reflect that?

After some deep thought, I realized it was time for a hairstyle update. I had been indecisive for months on how I wanted to change my hairstyle, but now I needed to own the fact that it had grown wild and needed taming. My hair was speaking "Help me," not "I can help you." A simple braiding style would keep me well groomed while I decided on a long-term solution for a haircut that fit my style.

What is your brand? Commit to developing your brand. Are you screaming "I'm stuck in the nineties," or are you so prim that your brand states you are untouchable? How can you update your brand to reflect who you are now? Or who you want to be?

Journal Notes

WEEK 45

Clean out your car

Our cars take us to all the places we need to go, to school, work, home, and recreation. Yet many of us have cars that look a mess on the inside. I have certainly been guilty of this myself. My car is often a reminder of what is going on in my life at the moment. When it's extremely busy at the office and home, my car usually looks like a small hurricane hit it.

One of the things I have noticed though is that when my car is clean and well organized I feel better. I feel closer to God and more in a grateful state of mind. Having an organized environment helps to provide focus and clarity. Yes a clean car can do all that.

So go ahead and clean your car out. Make a point of taking out trash daily and teaching the kids to do the same. Not only will you have a cleaner car but you will have taught your family members about the value of taking care of things that they own.

How will you incorporate this task into your life?

Journal Notes

Create a budget
that works

Recording your income and spending is a good start to having a clear idea of the current state of your finances. Much evidence points to the idea that money does not bring happiness. Yet many people believe that it does. Why the discrepancy? Research shows that individuals can be happy with less money as long as they feel in control of their finances. Many financial crises arise from poor financial planning, out-of-control spending, and helping others from a place of deficiency rather than a place of abundance.

Having dealt with many personality types over the years, I also know that budgeting is difficult for givers and entrepreneurs. If this is you, then make a simple habit of paying yourself first. Simply have your savings, retirement, and/or vacation money automatically deducted from your checking account each month. Making this small change will allow you to invest in yourself while living off of your balance.

Another empowering step in taking control of your financial future is to keep a balanced checkbook. Balance your checkbook every month to take control of your finances. Each month schedule a day on your calendar to review your budget and to go over your goals. This is a good opportunity to discover any patterns that are inconsistent with your intentions. By going over your financial records, you will recognize areas where you can eliminate wasteful spending and save more money. For example, I noticed that my family and

I ate out more during the winter season when the kids were active in sports. This reflection allowed me to organize our meals better and save money on multiple fast food runs during the week. Or you may find that you can eliminate services that you are not using such as club memberships and cable television upgrades.

This week create a budget for your weekly spending and a monthly financial budget. In addition to your budget, keep a record of where and how you spend your money.

What did you learn about yourself? According to your spending habits, what do you most value? How has creating this plan made you feel? In control? Abundant? Scarce? Examine your feelings and write them down.

Journal Notes

Clean out your email account

Sometime ago, I found myself completely over-whelmed by checking my email. I had tons of messages from my Facebook page, newsletters I subscribed to, and advertisements. It was bogging me down because most of it was irrelevant and cost me precious time every day. It took me hours to locate what I really needed in the moment.

Having an email system will help you to organize the way you manage your email. With so many things to do each day, it is easy to get lost in an abundance of messages. Here are a few strategies that I have implemented that may be helpful for you also. Make it a practice to separate your personal and business emails into separate folders or separate accounts altogether. My personal account is for family and friends only. Making this small but powerful change has saved me time and allowed me to enjoy reading my email again. Another great tool is to delete irrelevant messages as they pop up.

If your email account is full of old email, this step may take some time. Designate a few minutes each day to deleting old emails. Unsubscribe to things you do not read regularly. Organize important messages. For more help on organizing your account, you can use an online tool for creating and maintaining an email system. Two notable systems are active inbox and other inbox. Some email accounts such as Gmail have features that will sort your email into primary, social, and promotions categories.

What systems can you put into place to de-clutter your life? How has a system helped to simplify your life? Are you saving time?

Create a quiet space

Have you ever wanted a quiet retreat away from it all? Well you can create peaceful safe haven at your home. Having a space designated for reflection and creativity will serve you well.

Elizabeth Gilbert, the author of *Eat, Pray, Love,* went across the world in search of herself, but had a learning moment on *The Oprah Show* a few years ago when an audience member talked about the meditation space she created in her closet. She revealed that she was so inspired by Elizabeth's journey that she decided to create the space to remind her to take time for herself and to remember to hope and dream. Elizabeth along with the rest of us realized that a meditation space can be anywhere!

Are you short on space? Recently I talked to a young woman who had a long-term houseguest who took over her meditation room. She missed the feeling of having her quiet room. I suggested that she make her car her special place. On my advice, she cleaned her car and put her favorite guided meditation and musical CDs in her car. She even bought oils such as peppermint and sage to provide ambience. After work she would pull into the garage and spray her favorite scent and take a few minutes to meditate and pray before entering her house. Her car had become her sacred place. She later told me that her new quiet space had helped her in coping and healing just as much as the space she once occupied in her house. Remember, the Universe will support you in all your desires.

Do you have a designated space to pray, meditate, and to dream? If not, make a commitment to create one this week. Place special items in it such as your vision board, fresh flowers, and other items that inspire you to be your best. Use this space to refresh and rejuvenate yourself any time you need a lift. What changes have you recognized in your spiritual life since implementing this exercise?

Journal Notes

11

Purpose

"Many plans are in a man's mind, but it is the Lord's purpose for him that will stand."

PROVERB 19:21

Reconnect with your natural gifts

What are your natural gifts? These are talents that we provide or do with ease. You may notice that these specific gifts are often the ones that people ask of you. You may also notice that you are often inspired to lend your time in a certain way. Our gifts often lead us to our greater purpose in life. Discovering our gifts is a big part of our purpose here on earth. When we tap into our purpose, we give to humanity in the manner that God ordained us to. This feeling of living on purpose is so sweet that you will continue to want to repeat your actions over and over again to relive that feeling.

Begin to explore the following questions:

- What am I naturally good at?
- What am I often asked to do?
- When am I most joyful?
- In my free time, what do I want to do?
- If money were not an object, what would I do?
- Am I naturally an organizer and/or a giver?

I am a generous giver and it hurt not to be able to organize a fundraiser or to donate generously to my favorite charities after my car accident. One day I realized that I had to give what I could because I was ordained to be a giver under all circumstances. I decided to organize a clothing drive at my daughter's school for a homeless shelter. To my surprise, her teacher was delighted to help. She even enlisted the principal of the school. Within two months, we had collected tons of goods for the shelter. It felt so good to deliver the items, but it felt even better that this opportunity was shared with others. I would have never reached out to ask for help if I had the financial resources readily available. The students at the school learned a valuable lesson about giving and it was because I decided that I would use my talents in all situations.

This week write a list of things that you are naturally good at. What do you enjoy doing and would gladly do for free? How often are you doing this? What is holding you back? Rediscover your passion and purpose. What opportunities are in your community presently where you can lend your talent?

Journal Notes

Find your purpose and be true to yourself

This week I want you to look deep down inside. What is it that you have always wanted to do but somehow got sidetracked and never completed? Or what new opportunity has come your way but you just can't imagine it actually being successful? Today we are living in a world of unlimited possibilities. So rejoice. Get settled in and begin to visualize that thing that you have always desired coming true.

Many times we place limits on ourselves. We believe that we are not good enough, lack the proper resources, or are afraid of failure. These limiting beliefs will block you from achieving your purpose. Each day that you work on accomplishing your dreams and goals, you will move closer to living your purpose. The more you work on doing what you were called to do, the better you will become at it.

One of my favorite authors, Malcolm Gladwell, in his book *Outliers,* writes that it takes ten thousand hours to become excellent at something. So even the talented people that we all know of have worked at least ten thousand hours at their crafts. Make a decision today to work toward fulfilling your purpose each day. You will become better and better over time. Decide not to let that inner critic stop you from achieving your goals. You can do it!

During my period of uncertainty after my accident, I realized that I had placed limits on my life. I was not fully living the way God intended. I had attempted to write and publish a book several times, but I would always get derailed by one thing or another. But this time I decided that no matter what happened, or who even would eventually read this book, it was my story and I was going to write it. Please know this was not an easy task. I had just had my third child, in a new town and I was looking for employment daily. I had no one to turn to but God. So in spite of the uncertainty and through my daughter's nap and play time, I wrote every chance I got. This became the key to unlocking my soul and maintaining my value and worth when things were tough.

I encourage you my friend to listen to the beat of your own drum. What is it telling you? What are you most proud of? What would you like more time for? If I were to look at your life right now, what would I know about you? Sometimes the simple act of just observing can tell us so much.

Journal Notes

WEEK 51

Be in the moment

Each day this week, be mindful of your thinking. Work to be present throughout the day. This may be hard at first, but soon you will begin to experience peace as you become present in each moment. We live in a society where we are rewarded for being great multitaskers. But the truth is when we multitask we put additional stress on our body and brain. Not only does this affect our mental health, but it also affects how we interact with others. Our children, spouse, and friends may feel like we are not connected.

Being purposely mindful and present is good for you but it is equally beneficial for those who are experiencing us.

To put this into practice, I began leaving my cell phone in the car while attending games, school conferences, or plays. I wanted to be fully present. I knew it was too easy to look down at the phone. I also decided that dinnertime would be cell phone and television free zones. This practice was more difficult for my husband to incorporate. To help my husband get on track with staying in the moment, the girls began to stare at him until he said, "What." Then he would remember and place his phone to the side. It was these simple decisions that allowed our family to have a beautiful bonding experience. When many teenagers stop talking to their parents, our daughters told us everything and I do mean everything. Dinnertime in our home is quite festive with lively conversation of the day's happenings.

The Walking Meditation is a beautiful tool to incorporate so that you can began to live in the moment. Begin to walk outdoors observing nature. As you become mindful of God's creations and the majestic beauty of nature, you will naturally become more present. As you become more present, you will begin to sense a new inner peace and joy.

The main focus of the Walking Meditation is to observe and be fully aware of your body as it is in movement. Buddha was one of the first spiritual teachers to recognize and teach the significance of Walking Meditation. During Walking Meditation, walk slowly and purposely as you become attuned to the movement of your body and the feel of your weight on the ground. Walking meditation is wonderful for improving your focus and attention while being grounded. It also helps you to slow down and take in the beautiful power of now.

What will you do to become more mindful of this moment? What advances in technology take up a lot of your time?

WEEK 52

Emulate somebody

Everyone has a brave confident person in their circle either up close or from a distance. Do one thing that that person would do. You may have heard of Mrs. Taffi Dollar, of World Changers International Church, based in Atlanta, Georgia. Well, I remember the first time I heard her speak. I thought wow that lady is powerful and she truly embraces the power God gave her. She encouraged the crowd to stand on the word of God and stop being a wimp. I was inspired to stand up to fear and to do the things I was called to do. I am also blessed to have girlfriends in my circle that inspire me. Thea Camera, a mom and career woman, is also an aspiring actress. She hones her gift by acting in stage plays, commercials, and movies. Thea rekindled her love for acting while in her early forties. Her dedication to her craft has led to many notable roles. I am encouraged by Thea because she did not let her age, full-time career, or family life stop her from pursing her dreams.

There are so many women I could name, but I just wanted to say it doesn't matter where you are in life, you can make a change. So pick one thing that you admire about the women in your circle and begin to emulate their strengths. Maybe you desire to be gutsy, stronger, dress better, or eat healthier. Don't think about it, just do it. What qualities in others do you wish you had? Who can you emulate in your network of friends? What qualities do you possess that people would want to embody?

Personal Reflection

About the Author

Melisa Alaba divides her time between Chicago, Illinois and Atlanta, Georgia. She is a life coach, counselor, healer, and the founder and CEO of Vision Works Counseling and Coaching and the Pure Life Club. Additionally, Melisa is the co-founder of Women Entrepreneurs Rock an organization that supports women business owners. Melisa is an international speaker, who motivates audiences to live a life of abundance, peace, and purpose. She conducts meditation, abundance, and entrepreneur success workshops online and internationally. Melisa has also been featured as a healing

expert in *Ebony* magazine. Melisa is the proud mom of three beautiful daughters.

You can order Melisa's meditation CDs as a companion to this book. The CDs are based on Melisa's Pure Life Club classes. Both her book and CDs are available at her web-sites, www.visionworkscc.com, www.melisaalaba.com, www.purelifeclub.com, and on Amazon.com.

Praise For Melisa Alaba And Her Work

Laugh Out Loud is a well constructed guide to living by the eleven principles Alaba outlines with clarity and good sense. Easy to read and apply to your life, this books' unique take on self-help is a great read.

ANDREA WRIGHT,
author of *Trusting the Tingles* and *Her Essence in Death*

Live Out Loud is surely the ember to re-ignite the fire from within. Melisa uses her own life experiences to evoke us to a level of self awareness to live the life we desire. She speaks to the whole being and offers practical ways to achieve the ultimate. Chocked full of goodies- the framework used and if applied will undoubtedly lend to a life of fulfillment. Read it! Love it! Live it!!

SKYY BANKS,
Author of *Soul on Fire*